AEC REGENTS IN SERVICE

The Late 1960s and 1970s

David Christie

AMBERLEY

Probably my earliest non-preserved Regent photographed – although it's hardly 'in service'! Languishing in a scrapyard at Goodmayes, East London, is ex-Great Yarmouth Corporation EX 2877, one of a batch of five from 1931 with United bodies. Photographed in March 1971, this had been resident here since 1961 and was to survive until 1985, when it was purchased by the London Bus Museum at Cobham, where it was dismantled for spares. This image could be compared to the last one in this book.

First published 2019

Amberley Publishing
The Hill, Stroud
Gloucestershire, GL5 4EP

www.amberley-books.com

Copyright © David Christie, 2019

The right of David Christie to be identified as the Author of this work has been asserted in accordance with the Copyrights, Designs and Patents Act 1988.

ISBN 978 1 4456 8954 8 (print)
ISBN 978 1 4456 8955 5 (ebook)

British Library Cataloguing in Publication Data.
A catalogue record for this book is available from the British Library.

Origination by Amberley Publishing.
Printed in the UK.

Contents

Introduction

As a 'companion' to my book on Leyland PD Titans, this collection is of the AEC Regent family as recorded on my trips around Britain.

It all started in May 1967 when I found Routemasters on my local 86 route Sunday service – that is, in Romford, on the eastern outskirts of London. Panic ensued and the camera I had purchased to record dying BR steam in 1962 was now turned to photographing London RTs. As it happened, the RT was to soldier on for another twelve years – but that's another story! Meanwhile, I soon found that my horizons broadened to include buses other than London Transport, and started to travel ever increasing distances from the south coast up to Teeside and over to the Isle of Man. The Western Counties were omitted through higher priorities nearer to hand, as was Wales – not through any lack of visiting, but through a lack of Regents.

My task was to seek out the last traditional exposed-radiator buses in service, which, at that time, were fast on their way out. First among the various makes surviving was the AEC Regent III, which, with its distinctive triangular-badged radiator, had always been a favourite of mine.

The earlier Regent II was encountered very infrequently, usually as a trainer or works vehicle, as was the original Mk I – but then there were many of these produced so these were more likely to crop up than their Mk II successor. I am afraid that the final Regent variant, the Mark V, got short shrift from my camera to begin with (as it was an enclosed-radiator design), but later in the period covered in this book it began to be considered more favourably.

The first Regent was produced in 1929 and was designed by J. G. Rackham, who had 'switched camps' from Leyland, where he had been responsible for the groundbreaking Titan TD a few years earlier. The Regent was a development of that Titan, being of a more compact layout with a new 7.7-litre AEC engine and transmission. Many thousands were built, becoming London's standard pre-war ST and STL classes. The Mark II Regent was built from 1945 to 1947 and was a 'stopgap' model, with only 700 being produced before the legendary Mk III appeared.

In the meantime, London's RT class had been developed with its revolutionary ideas in 1938, but only 150 odd were built due to wartime restrictions. Come 1947, however, the design was further developed into the post-war standard London RT with a 9.6-litre engine. Some 4,670 were built for London, with 100 odd going to 'provincial' customers, the design generally being considered too expensive and elaborate outside of the capital. But these customers now had the standard Mark III available, built from 1947 to 1954, which proved a winner and appeared nationwide.

Mention must be made of the Mark IV, which was a one-off experimental vehicle with an underfloor engine that was seen before the Mark V appeared in 1954. Although the new enclosed-radiator design was generally the norm, the exposed radiator could still be specified if preferred. The Mark V finished production in 1969, thus ending one of Britain's most renowned bus families.

The lion's share of the enclosed images come from the Isle of Man, with Douglas Corporation's wonderful primrose and maroon livery portrayed. These were courtesy of several weeks' holidays on the island over a ten-year period. Bradford, Ipswich and Brighton yielded more Regents than most, with the contrasting Weymann and Park Royal body treatments in Brighton and Ipswich respectively. These two feature on this book's cover and I would be so bold as to venture that Ipswich No. 1 is the ideal Regent portrayed in service in this book! Bradford's own Weymann Regents were bolstered by ex-London RTs – a feature throughout this book.

London Transport itself is given just a representative section as the LT area (mainly Central and East London) is covered in my previous books. Unfortunately Essex operators are unavoidably duplicated, as are the Isle of Man Regents – the latter featuring in my recent all-island book. I have tried to keep this to a minimum, with the LT section, for instance, having only a few images previously published.

The final few images are from Scotland and are the only ones taken of Regents there. They were never a popular model in the country, the single-deck Regal variety being more favoured. My abode actually shifted from Essex to central Scotland in 1973, but it was generally too late by then to find much of interest for the traditional enthusiast. The very last image is of a preserved Regent – the earliest I could find – to represent the Regent at its best.

This book, then, is my tribute to one of Britain's most famous buses – and my personal favourite too.

David Christie

London Transport

A representative selection, mainly of the 'standard' RT and RLH Regents, showing the different livery variants.

The 'standard' RT – a Mk III with Park Royal or Weymann bodywork to LT design, built from 1947 to 1954. Bodies and chassis were interchangeable and were often swapped around at overhaul, making it difficult to date the bus from its fleet number. Here is RT4377 at the Becontree Heath terminus of route 9, photographed in September 1967. This example shows the cream between-decks relief band, which was phased out on overhaul from 1965.

The first 750 bodies were built in 1947–48 to this 'top-box' configuration, where the route number was placed in a box on the front dome, with correspondingly different 'via' and final destination blinds lower down. More space was available for the front adverts, which wrapped round to the sides on the more numerous type without top boxes. RT908 is pictured here on a very quiet Sunday in June 1968 at Romford crossroads – my home town until 1973. All top boxes were gone by June 1970.

Standard RT4542, seen at Farningham in May 1967, showing the 'mist grey' between-decks band replacement colour, which started to be applied on overhaul from 1965. I always preferred the cream – but then cream was fast becoming a rare colour on buses and coaches in general; it's only quite recently that it has been making a comeback. The last red RT ran in public service in April 1979, but two were kept as 'skid-buses' into 1980.

The country division of London Transport used exactly the same RT types, although the top-box variant went much earlier than its red counterpart – by 1964, too early for my camera. So here is RT3450 at Gravesend in April 1968, in typical Country condition, with a cream relief band. This was to remain unchanged until London Country split in January 1970. Other than that cream band the whole bus was green – including the mudguards and wheels – which in my opinion would have looked better in black and Tuscan red, as per the red buses.

As mentioned above, London Country was formed in January 1970, but at first the only change visible on the RTs was the new fleet name on the side and the overpainting of the triangular radiator badge. Gradually yellow relief bands appeared, then some visited LT's Aldenham works for the last time for a complete overhaul and re-emerged looking like new. RT3051 is one such example, and is seen here at Aveley Usk Road in March 1971. The last London Country RT in service ran in June 1978, with six still being used as trainers etc. into 1980.

The final RT livery, being the Green Line coach version – like a country green bus but with a light green relief band – and no adverts. The Green Line symbol appeared on each side, originally as a raised metal motif, but when most Green Line RTs were replaced by Routemasters from 1965, this symbol was just painted on the remaining RTs. Seen at Aldgate terminus in September 1967 is RT999, which was kept in superb condition by Romford London Road garage – which had only nine for use on the 'rush hour' 722. This service closed in August 1968.

The other type of Regent operated by LT was the definitely non-standard RLH. A lowbridge design was needed post-war and the opportunity was taken to purchase twenty of a batch of Regent IIIs with lowbridge Weymann bodies over-ordered by Midland General in 1950. A further fifty-six almost identical vehicles were added in 1952, making a total of seventy-six operated. Being a non-LT design these buses always looked odd among the RTs. Here is RLH60 at Wealdstone on the 230 route, in October 1968. This was a cream-banded example.

RLH74, again on the 230 route at Wealdstone, but in July 1968, portrays the grey relief band. The RLHs lasted in service until April 1971, but many have survived, with over 50 per cent being exported to the USA – no doubt as a typical London bus!

The country area RLH differed from the red version in the same way as the RT, which can be seen as RLH36 arrives at the Ripley terminus of the 436A. Photographed here in June 1969, this RLH shows up its red examples on the previous page by sporting a radiator badge – an unusual omission on the Central buses.

This is my only photograph of a non-preserved (at the time) STL, and was taken at Mulley's Yard, Ixworth, Suffolk, in May 1968. EGO 426 was STL2377 and is now, happily, preserved and restored (completed in 2000) to its London state. It has an LPTB body and dates back to 1937, and was in service until 1953 at my 'local' garage – Hornchurch. It ran for Mulley's until 1961, but since then had been deteriorating, not being finally rescued until 1988 by the London Bus Museum. This totally unexpected find was one of several elderly buses and coaches spread around Jack Mulley's yard. Jack was an enthusiast himself and was always ready to chat.

Spread throughout LT land were the incredible 'Tenders' and the like from the CDS fleet. 832J (JJ 4379), photographed at Neasden depot in July 1968, was ex-STL162, dating from 1933 and converted to a Tender in 1950. It was retired in 1978 and is now preserved. Just look at all those bonnet-side louvres!

The palm, however, for the earliest Regent in service must go to preserved 1930-built ST922 with its outside-staircase Tilling body. In 1972 it was hired back by LT from its private owner to operate the Tourist Route 100. As LT had various elderly preserved buses of its own, it seems odd that one of these was not used. The history of ST922 is that it was built for Thomas Tilling and was taken into LT stock with the formation of that company in 1933. It was in service until 1946, and was then used as a mobile canteen until 1954, being then 'disposed of'. The final important date was 1966, when preservation began. It was still going strong on Route 100 when last seen by myself in 1977, but here it is seen on its inaugural run, on 9 April 1972, on Westminster Bridge.

Greater London Operators (East)

The Independent operators in the eastern Greater London boroughs invariably used ex-LT RTs – as far as the AEC marque was concerned – the various variants of the RT carry on from the last section.

Upminster & District ran several stage carriage services, but their buses could be found anywhere in the Hornchurch and Romford areas, running on school services and private work. Ex-London RTs were the favourite AECs, being operated in a dark blue and cream livery. Here is MXX39 (ex-RT2951), dating from 1952 but with an earlier roofbox body fitted. This early design (designated 3RT3) was instantly recognisable from its deeper valance over the bonnet space, incorporating the between-decks relief band. Private operators seemed to be in the habit of removing that roofbox, as here. Occasionally platform doors were fitted, again as on MXX39. This RT was purchased from LT in 1965 and ran for its new owners until October 1970. It is pictured here near Corbets Tey in November 1969.

The colours and fleet name of Upminster & District changed during 1970 with a reincarnation of the City Coach Co., which famously ran the London Wood Green to Southend route up until 1952. KLB 773 is ex-RT2394 and has a Saunders body (which was one of the companies that catered for the demand in RT bodies outside of the normal suppliers, with 300 being built). The only visible external difference on these was the offside route number fixing (disused since 1963/4), which was set further back than the norm. KLB 773 was new in 1949 and was purchased by City in April 1970, and ran for them until October 1972. It is pictured here at Upminster station in May 1970. The bus looked very smart at first glance, but why, oh why was there a blindspot with the paper adverts?

The City livery application has weathered somewhat in this portrayal of KLB 762 (ex-RT2383) in March 1971 at its 'Optimist' Hornchurch terminus. The worst thing about it was that the paint had been applied around the old paper adverts that had been there when the bus was LT red, so now the original livery was showing through! KLB 762 was in use from 1949; it was purchased by City in July 1970 and withdrawn in October 1972.

The next livery/name change from 'City' was to 'Blue Line', which came with a rather unusual shade of blue. NXP 949 (ex-RT4807) is seen here just outside of the Upminster Bridge depot in January 1972. This RT was new in 1954 and entered the Blue Line fleet in April 1971. I have no record of its disposal date but should imagine it followed the two-year pattern. This was my last experience of this ever-changing company as my move north prohibited further exposure.

A livery familiar to boys from the 1950s was Matchbox Toys, and their box colours were replicated on their works buses. Awaiting the factory whistle at their Hackney works in August 1968 is JXN345 (ex-RT944), which dates from 1948 and was fitted with an early 3RT3 body before being disposed of in 1964 – eventually ending up with Lesneys, the Matchbox proprietors, in 1966. This one has had its roofbox removed.

Elm Park Coaches was a small company situated in Oldchurch Road, Romford. This RT was the only ex-London vehicle known to me – as well as the only bus in the fleet not still in its original livery. LYR 731 (ex-RT2747) was another case of an old 3RT3 body being fitted onto a later 1951 chassis, but this one still retained its roofbox. Purchased in 1964 from LT, it went, surprisingly, to Upminster & District in January 1968. It is shown here at Elm Park's depot in October 1967.

KGK 721 (ex-RT1462) wears a similar colour scheme to the Elm Park bus but is a very different RT variant, being one of the 120 RT bodies built by Cravens. In their case, they comprised standard Cravens bodies modified to look like a standard RT. There were five, not four, downstairs windows, the front profile was much more upright with smaller top windows and there was a distinctly curved back end. They were also built with a top box, but it has been removed on this example. KGK721 dates from 1949, being withdrawn by LT in 1957 but not getting to Red Car Hire Service of Chigwell until September 1965. It was photographed at Marks Gate in May 1969.

KYY 588 (ex-RT1750) lines up with LYY 737 (ex-RTL767) at Walden's Epping depot in March 1970. The RT was built in 1950 with a Saunders body and was with Walden's from January 1969 to November 1971.

East Anglia

The main operators using Regents, shown here, spreading out from my base in Romford, were that devotee of the second-hand LT bus, Osborne's, Colchester Corporation, the all-AEC Ipswich Corporation, and Lowestoft Corporation.

Southend Corporation

This view is of one of the six Regents (dating from 1950 with typical curvaceous Massey bodywork) that operated in an eighty-strong fleet dominated by Leylands and Daimlers. The whole batch was withdrawn in 1965 but this one escaped scrapping and was obviously being renovated when seen parked in a pub's car park at Rayleigh Weir on 23 April 1968. Although showing the registration EHJ 443, that bus had been scrapped. What had happened was that the radiator, complete with the affixed registration plate, was transferred to EHJ 445 (fleet number 261), so hopefully someone noticed and repainted the last digit of the offending plate before the bus (now fitted with platform doors) took off on its intended world tour.

Osbourne's of Tollesbury

A visit to the little village of Tollesbury, Essex, in 1969 produced what appeared to be a wholly ex-London fleet. Early RFs and RTs abounded – most in an attractive variation of LT red. Arriving in the village square on the Maldon service is their No. 39 (ex-RT2827), a 1952 bus with an early 3RT3 body. This had been withdrawn by LT in June 1965 and stayed with Osborne's until June 1972. It will be seen that platform doors had been fitted and Osborne's own little circular flashing indicator 'ears' had taken the place of the LT design. The three black-edged cream strips were a real touch of brilliance – a livery that LT could have had! All in all, this was a very smart bus just let down by the usual affliction – a bashed top dome. All Osborne's photographs were taken on 8 March 1969.

No. 39 rounds the corner at Tolleshunt D'Arcy on its way to Maldon. Upon withdrawal in 1972 it was purchased for preservation, still in its Osborne's livery, at Castle Point Museum, Canvey Island.

Back in Tollesbury village, No. 21 (ex-RT3671) is seen passing through the main street. This was a February 1953 build, and was again fitted with an earlier body. It was with Osborne's from February 1964 to June 1971.

No. 21 has now reached the depot at Tollesbury. This view shows how well those ivory/cream bands had been applied, and on this bus the dumb irons appear to be red. It's a pity about that dome!

A final view of Osborne's No. 21, from which it will be seen that the original open platform has been retained.

Colchester Corporation

Two batches of Regents were operated by Colchester, but the earlier 1947 class of four had gone by my visits in 1967, where I found two of the three still working from the 1953 batch. These had Massey bodywork. Seen here at the station stop in September 1967 is No. 12. Note the attractive shaded fleet numbers. No. 12 was withdrawn in April 1971.

Colchester No. 10 at the entrance to the bus station, photographed in September 1967.

No. 10 at the bus station in March 1969. Something strange has happened to its nearside mudguard. No. 10 was withdrawn in January 1971.

Norfolk's of Nayland

Norfolk's were one of the independents running into Colchester, and on 1 July 1967 their TWL 928, an ex-City of Oxford 1953 Regent III with a Park Royal body, arrives in the city. For a second-hand bus it was looking very well kept, with none of your 'usual' bashes. It ran for Norfolk's until February 1972, when it was acquired for preservation, being put back into its original Oxford livery.

Ipswich Corporation

This was a remarkable fleet being all AEC and not having a motorbus until 1950, trolleybuses being all-present up till then. A first order for six Regents was followed by four in 1954 and two in 1955 with a final four of the Mk III in 1956. From 1957 Mk Vs expanded the orders with thirty-seven up to 1962. Pictured at the Bourne Bridge terminus in September 1967 is Park Royal-bodied No. 6 from the 1950 batch. Note the unusual short section of rain strips over two of the lower-deck windows, and also the lovely shaded fleet numerals. No. 6 was withdrawn in March 1969.

No. 1 herself, a favourite combination of Regent III and Park Royal, heads for Bourne Bridge. Trolleybus standards are still well in evidence, the closure having taken place in 1963. This and the next three photographs were taken in September 1967.

No. 22, with an RT-influenced Park Royal body, is from the batch of four Mk IIIs built in 1954. It enters The Square, heading for the airport.

No. 1 again, seen crossing the railway tracks at Ipswich Docks. She was in service until June 1973, when she was bought for preservation at the Ipswich Transport Museum.

No. 22 at The Square. This image shows the rather outdated semaphore direction arms in action well – a surprising feature to still be in use in 1967.

No. 15, from the 1954-built batch of four, turns into The Square in March 1969.

This bus was duly 'chased' and an opportunity to photograph by the gasworks was used here.

The final shot of No. 15 near its Gainsborough terminus. Note the many trolley standards still standing – now in use as road lighting.

Mulley's (Longlands)

Mulley's were an independent company that seemed to double as a transport museum, such was the contents of their depot at Ixworth, Suffolk. Already seen in the LT section was a pre-war London STL. Not so old (the gems fall outside the scope of this book) but still ex-LT was KGK 773 (ex-RT1514) – a Cravens-bodied RT from 1950 in the green livery of Langland's (part of Mulley's). The usual habit of lopping off the top box had been carried out. This RT was sold off by LT in August 1956 but was not withdrawn by Mulley's until June 1969; apparently, it wasn't scrapped until 1975. It was seen here in May 1968.

Another Longlands vehicle at Ixworth was 1949 Weymann-bodied HER 29. It was new to Fisons Pest Control, Cambridge, which changed hands in 1958. Apart from needing a good wash it looked quite serviceable, but I do not know its history beyond my photograph, which was taken in May 1968.

Lowestoft Corporation

Lowestoft had a very small fleet of just seventeen vehicles, with a batch of nine Mk II Regents built in 1947 that had, most unusually, Eastern Coachworks bodies. These were the only type that I saw running on my one visit on 11 October 1969. No. 21, seen here on the outskirts of the town, was eventually preserved at the East Anglian Transport Museum. The whole batch was withdrawn from service in June 1971.

No. 22 stops near the harbour, where the driver chats with a colleague.

No. 26, passing a policeman in Sea Road.

No. 22 leaves Sea Road and turns into Main Road. The splendid array of louvres and circular ventilation holes on the engine compartment side are well seen here – such a contrast to the blank-sided Regent III.

No. 25 crosses the Harbour swing bridge in glorious weather.

No. 22 turns right across the main street with some interested youngsters on the top deck.

No. 25 at the Pakefield terminus. The very 'square' ECW body is accentuated by the highbridge design.

South Coast

This section is mainly comprised of the two near-neighbour resorts Eastbourne and Brighton, as they have most of the Regents on the coast. There is only one image from the traditional Provincial fleet and a couple from Southampton – Regent Vs no less. Bournemouth scrapes in by virtue of a tower wagon conversion from a bus.

Eastbourne Corporation
Roughly 50 per cent of Eastbourne's fleet of around fifty-six were Regents, with the largest batch of eight, dating from 1951, having Bruce/East Lancs bodies. No. 46, pictured here, lets the side down somewhat, with the fleet's usual smart appearance being marred by bumper and radiator damage. This photograph was taken in September 1967, and the bus was withdrawn in February 1971.

No. 43 is seen at the railway station stop. Note that the adverts are painted on – no messy paper stickers here, although they could have gone the whole hog and had none at all. Seen in September 1967, the bus was withdrawn in October 1970.

Numerically, No. 48 was the last of the batch, but it was the first to go – in July 1970. It is pictured here in the Old Town in September 1967.

The last photograph of my 1967 visit, with No. 43 in the Old Town. Full use has been made of the rear advertising space – but paper stickers have appeared to spoil the effect. The rather large fleet number is noticeable.

A few years later, in July 1970, No. 45 is seen passing an open-top Southdown bus in a busy scene near the station. Despite the paper adverts, the bus still looks pretty smart, but it only had four more months left to run in service.

Again photographed in July 1970, No. 46 has paper ads but, strangely, none at the front. The bumper damage shown in my first 1967 shot had been repaired, but not the radiator. No. 46 would be withdrawn in April 1971.

Brighton Corporation

Brighton Corporation's fleet was primarily made up of trolleybuses in the late 1950s (fifty-two in number), with a pre-war and a post-war batch of Regents totalling only ten and fourteen respectively. The trolleys went in 1961 but were replaced by Leylands, leaving the 1947–49 batch of AECs to be seen on my 1967/8 visits. This Regent III/Weymann combination seemed to fit so well – notwithstanding the corporation's totally 'over the top' advert applications! No. 89, pictured here at the Steine in September 1967, was from 1949 and showed a different 'face' to the rest of the class, with a Regent radiator inscription and the number plate set higher.

Also on my September 1967 visit, Nos 88 (1947) and 90 (1949) are seen amid a fairly representative collection of British cars. Somebody has been overzealous when pasting ads on the bus behind, with one even creeping round to the front. Thankfully, this wasn't seen repeated elsewhere. No. 88 was withdrawn in December 1968, and No. 90 went in April 1969.

No. 91 climbs and turns at Elm Grove in the last summer of Regent operation, in June 1968. The full effect of the advertising is shown here.

No. 91 at the Steine in June 1968.

A rare instance of capturing front and back views in the same shot – and of the only two Regents seen in service that day; namely, Nos 91 and 93 on 30 June 1968 at Elm Grove.

No. 92 (1949) passes the fountains near the Steine in September 1967. This bus was withdrawn in 1969.

No. 91 is seen on a dual carriageway in Brighton in June 1968.

No. 93, also photographed in June 1968, pulls out from a stop near the Steine.

Provincial (Gosport & Fareham)

This rather unusual collection of around seventy vehicles at one time had 50 per cent of its fleet as Regents – and all pre-war at that. But that was in the late 1950s, since when Guy Arabs have predominated. Re-bodying by Reading was rife, but by the mid-1950s new bodies with their raked-back appearance looked almost as though they could have been originals. Pictured at Gosport Ferry on 6 September 1967 is one such example – Regent No. 34, dating from 1936 with a 1956 body. It was withdrawn in September 1970. Sister bus No. 35 has been saved for preservation. Unfortunately, this is my only shot of a Provincial AEC in service.

City of Southampton

After the withdrawal of their fine fleet of Guy Arabs, the city was left with a preference for Regent Vs – some eighty being delivered from 1962 to 1967, most with attractive East Lancs-based bodies. My 1975 visit was mainly for ship interest, so only a few buses were photographed. Nevertheless, here we see No. 373, built in 1966 with a Neepsend/East Lancs body, in a deserted High Street on Sunday 6 July 1975. It was withdrawn in 1980.

From the same batch as above, No. 380 makes a good comparison with the 1963-built Leyland PD 2A/37 behind, with its awful Leyland front end and its box-like Park Royal body.

Bournemouth Corporation

This vehicle may have been the only AEC in the Bournemouth fleet, a conversion in 1948 of an ex-Huddersfield 1934 Regent to a tower wagon, intended to service trolleybus wiring. It is seen here exiting Mallard Road depot on 26 January 1969, still at work. The trolley system closed in April 1969, and VH 6217 finally ended its working life in May 1970. It was then bought for preservation.

Reading to the Midlands

Starting from Reading, with its batch of the last Regent III's to be built, then up to the city of Oxford with that fantastic livery, and the small Independent, Charlton-on-Otmoor. At last into the real Midlands with the city of Nottingham and West Bridgford, and its almost all-AEC tiny fleet.

Reading Corporation

Reading's Regents were the last Regent IIIs to be built and comprised a batch of four from 1956 (a follow-on from its 1955 batch of five). These had Park Royal lowbridge bodies with platform doors. Four of these were parked at the depot in July 1970 – Nos 98, 1, 99 and 4. Some strange withdrawal dates have been recorded for this class, with these four covering from August 1971 to January 1991 – adding to which three (including Nos 98 and 4) have been preserved.

No. 3 turns across the road at Reading General station in September 1967. It passes under the trolleybus wiring as it goes, which at the time was still in use, the system closing in November 1968. Note the platform doors, which were specified for all of Reading's fleet. No. 3 went on to be preserved after withdrawal in April 1987.

No. 3 again, parked up at the depot with Crossley No. 93 for a comparison of styles.

Mill Lane depot in July 1970, with possibly seven of the class assembled. To the fore are Nos 96, 2 and 100. These three had more normal withdrawal dates, from 1973 to 1976.

No. 3 was singled out from the above as it had recently undergone a repaint, which was nice to see on a fourteen-year-old vehicle.

City of Oxford

A single visit to see this wonderful livery, and the beautifully kept vehicles, wasn't enough. The city of Oxford had an almost 100 per cent AEC fleet at the time, with Regent Vs in both the exposed and enclosed-radiator styles. I was unfortunately too late to see the Mk IIIs, but at least one exposed-radiator Mk V, No. 954 from 1957 with Weymann body, was photographed – seen here in Saint Aldgate's Street on 1 August 1970. In total there were sixty-four Mk Vs in the fleet.

My reluctance to photograph anything other than exposed-radiator types was, later, a regretted decision, but occasionally I made an exception, as per No. 974 here. This vehicle dates from 1958 and has Park Royal bodywork. It was withdrawn only one month after this shot was taken, but it was saved for preservation.

No. 954 again, this time in the High Street. This was the only exposed-radiator Mk V I saw that day. It was withdrawn in August 1971.

Charlton-on-Otmoor Services

This was a small independent based a few miles north of Oxford. At the bus station in August 1970 is HLX 215, an ex-LT RT398 from 1948 with original RT3 body. It was bought from LT in 1964 and served with its second owner until 1996 – exactly twice as long as with LT. It was certainly kept in superb condition when seen here in its attractive two-tone blue livery.

HLX 215 catches the sunlight in a nearside view; it's a shame about the top dome 'bash' – an almost expected feature of second-hand vehicles. It is surprising here though, in view of the vehicle's otherwise well-kept condition.

Nottingham City

Nottingham City's fleet was another of those that were predominately AEC, with almost 200 Mk IIIs operating in the mid-1960s followed up by sixty-three Mk Vs. Among these were just ten lowbridge examples, which were 1954-built Mark IIIs with Park Royal bodywork. No. 203 is shown here leaving Broadmarsh bus station on 24 April 1969 – the date for all my Nottingham shots.

Another lowbridge Mk III, No. 208, is in Wheeler Gate. This small class were all gone by June 1971.

The large batch of 1953/4 Mk IIIs were, by the time of my visit, fairly well decimated, so I was pleased to see No. 181 in Long Row. Only two of the class were left by the end of 1969, but second-hand examples were still to be seen in Hull. As usual, bodywork is by Park Royal.

Two of the exposed-radiator Mk Vs from 1955, Nos 225 and 232, in Long Row. Withdrawal of these came in 1971.

A closer look at No. 225 at its stop in Long Row.

West Bridgford UDC

Almost part of Nottingham, West Bridgford UDC buses were in fact taken over by the city in September 1968. Despite this, on my 24 April 1969 visit I found the old attractive livery unchanged. It was only a small fleet (twenty-eight in the mid-1960s) and of all-AEC manufacture. Seen here in Wheeler Gate in Nottingham is one of the handful of 1948-built Regent IIIs, No. 175, which has a Park Royal body.

No. 175 again, seen here turning into Broadmarsh bus station. These Regents were withdrawn in September – just a few months away. Presumably that's why they were never repainted.

No. 171, in much better light in Melton Road. There is no mistaking this bus's destination!

No. 171 at the Melton Road terminus. The old-fashioned triangular stop light is noticeable, as is the registration number in the rear window. The combination of this particular style of Park Royal body and AEC make this my favourite type of bus – alongside the Ipswich one seen earlier in this book.

North

This section starts in the west at Liverpool with its huge numbers of Regents sadly mainly reduced to 'tin-fronts' by the 1970s. Heading due east, the next call is at Leigh Corporation (near Wigan) with its small fleet of sixty easily overlooked. Bypassing Manchester and its environs, which totally shunned AECs, and up to a smart fleet of Regents at Huddersfield before reaching Bradford with its trolleys and mainly AEC fleet, including ex-London RTs. A short step then to the city of Leeds with its large numbers of Regent Vs. The last call is on the east coast at Hull to find ex-Nottingham Regents and ex-St Helens RTs – all in a very strange livery!

Liverpool

Heading over the old tram tracks (closed 1957) at Pier Head in June 1967 is Regent III No. A532. One of a batch of sixty from 1948, they had Weymann-framed bodies finished by the corporation, giving them a narrow, gaunt appearance. This one was withdrawn in January 1968.

A747 was from the larger batch of 100 1950-built Regent IIIs, and in this example the Weymann frames were finished by Aero & Eng. The drab green livery and black-painted radiator did not impress – although at least this one had an AEC triangular badge adorning is radiator, as well as 'Regent' scroll, which is barely noticeable. Photographed in February 1968 at the Speke Estate terminus, A747 was withdrawn two months later, in April.

From a batch of almost 200 Regent Vs, A116, with its Crossley body, dates form 1955. This then was the operator-inspired tin-front look, which would have looked far better had the standard Mk V bonnet grille been used instead. A116 is at Pier Head in April 1970, and the bus was withdrawn in March 1972.

A116 is passed by a Leyland tin-front, which manages to look even worse than the AEC!

Leigh Corporation

Leigh Corporation ran a small fleet, which included a batch of seven 1953-built Mk IIIs with East Lancs lowbridge bodies. Here is No. 6943, which is seen entering Leigh bus station. The three-banded cream relief livery was heartening after the Liverpool experience, but the painted radiator surround was unfortunate. All Leigh shots were taken on 3 August 1970.

No. 6945 leaves the bus station, showing the beautifully presented corporation name and crest on its side. The East Lancs bodies looked good and were well proportioned.

No. 6942 in Leigh town centre.

Huddersfield Corporation

Huddersfield Corporation had a very smart fleet, with the two narrow cream bands accentuating the wide waistband. There were fifty-six Regents in the fleet in the mid-1960s, which had been provided in small batches. No. 234, a Regent III with an East Lancs lowbridge body, was one of twelve built in 1954. It is seen here in the Main Street. No. 234 was to last another three years. All Huddersfield photographs were taken on 25 April 1969.

No. 234 again, parked in St George Square. Note the 'leaning-back' old trolley standard prominent – the trolley system having closed in July 1968.

A different view of No. 234 in St George Square. The use of the town's name alone on the side of the bus was unusual.

An earlier Regent III – No. 173 from 1951, with a highbridge East Lancs body. Again, this bus came from a batch of twelve. No. 173 was withdrawn in May 1970.

No. 183, a Regent V from 1958, was a departure body-wise, having a Roe body. It was one of a batch of eight.

No. 243, from the 1954 batch, but tipping over into 1955, is seen turning into the main street.

Bradford Corporation

With the last trolleybus system in Britain, Bradford was visited several times. The bus fleet, pre-Atlantean, had a predominantly AEC make-up, with a large contingent of front-entrance 1960s Regent Vs. For more variety there were the twenty-five RTs bought from London Transport in 1958. First for attraction, however, were the batch of forty Regent IIIs, of which No. 33 is shown entering Town Hall Roundabout in April 1969. No. 33 dates from 1950 and has a Weymann body.

No. 33 again, under the trolleybus wiring (the system didn't close until March 1972). There were not many of this batch left in service and I only saw two, and both of these were withdrawn in January 1970. No. 33 was photographed in April 1969.

My first view of an ex-London RT was somewhat incomplete – at Town Hall Square, in April 1969. No. 413 had been RT177 (1947) with an early RT3 body. Having had the roofbox expertly removed, it had also been given new destination screens.

This RT does not have an early body, surprisingly, and still has the LT destination screens intact. No. 401 dates from 1947 and is ex-RT154. The 1958 purchase date meant that LT-style flashing direction indicator 'ears' were still to come.

No. 401 again, this time near Thornbury. Despite the rather dishevelled appearance, the livery suited the RTs well, and one has been preserved as such. Photographed in April 1969, the two RTs featured would be withdrawn in August of that year, so this was to be my only opportunity to see them.

One of the large batch of sixty Regent Vs dating from 1963 with Metro-Cammell bodywork, No. 145 is at Town Hall Square on the trolleybus closure weekend. Note the RT-like rear wheel discs.

Inside Thornbury depot on 25 March 1972, the tram tracks are still in situ. In the middle of the photograph is No. 137, another 1963 Regent V from the same batch as the previous shot.

No. 13, a 1949-built Regent III with a Weymann body, takes in the view at the old Buttershaw depot. One of the delights of Bradford was that most routes climbed up out of the city to give grand views. No. 13 was photographed in April 1969 and withdrawn in January 1970.

Leeds City Transport

Leeds buses were different – perhaps it was the livery, or the stainless steel unpainted bonnet sides? However, they had a varied fleet. Leylands and Daimlers featured in good numbers, but it was the Regents that won hands down with over 350 buses – almost half the fleet. Here, somewhere west of Leeds, is No. 734 – one of a batch of thirty Regent IIIs with Roe bodies built in 1954. This one was withdrawn in August 1970. It was photographed on 25 April 1969, the date on which all of my Leeds images were taken.

No. 845 was one of the 135-strong batch of Regent Vs built in 1956/7 with very similar Roe bodies. The lack of upper front window vents was the usual difference. It is seen here near Westgate. Withdrawal came in May 1971.

No. 860, from the same batch as the previous shot, is again seen near Westgate. This one has a curious aluminium shield attached to its radiator, and was withdrawn in July 1971.

A Regent III from the 1954 batch, No. 750 is seen at the Saint Peters roundabout. A queue of buses forms in the background. This was another August 1970 withdrawal.

One of the small batch of late Regent Vs from 1958 with reverse registrations, No. 896 is seen at the Corn Exchange, with its domes, spires and a wonderful old street lamp.

No. 656, one of a 7-foot 6-inch-wide-bodied batch of Regent IIIs from 1952, is seen at Bridge End. Visible at the far right of the picture is a bus with a different style of fleet name, which is displayed nearer the front end. No doubt No. 656 never came to wear this, being withdrawn just five months later.

The oldest Leeds bus seen that day was No. 617. Dating from 1950, it does look a little different in its Roe body style in that there are no upper deck front ventilators and the lighter green relief canopy band over the engine compartment is deeper. It carries that radiator blanking seen earlier. It is arriving at Saint Peter's bus station and passing a curiosity – a Guy Wulfrunian of West Riding. It's surprising that No. 617 lasted as long as some of the Regent Vs, into 1971.

Kingston-upon-Hull Corporation

Certainly an unusual fleet – with its 'streamline' livery and many second-hand buses in service. At the depot are a mixture of ex-Saint Helens RTs and ex-Nottingham Regents. Nos 1, 2 and 4 are ex-Saint Helens No. 134 (1952), No. 152 (1950) and No. 149. The bus in the middle is No. 156, while the last in line is No. 154, both were ex-Nottingham (1954). The photograph was taken on 7 August 1970, as were all shots taken in Hull. Most of this line-up was withdrawn in 1971.

Ex-Nottingham Regent IIIs with Park Royal bodies, Hull Nos 178 and 181 are seen in the town centre. Thirty-five of these were purchased.

Ex-Nottingham No. 158 leaves the bus station.

Inside the depot with a close-up of 1952-built ex-Saint Helens BDJ 815 (Hull No. 132). This batch of nineteen were identical to the London RT, except the destination screens had been modified in Hull. The mismatched headlights were rather unfortunate.

A survivor from the 1946 batch of Regent IIs with Weymann bodies is HAT 245, seen in use by the Engineering Department. Its side windows have been replaced. This is a rare survivor indeed, as it is now preserved.

East Yorkshire

The Regents in this fleet had specially adapted bodies to enable them to pass under the 'Beverley Bar'. Not exactly a livery to brighten up the place! Here is No. 690, a Regent V with a Willowbrook body. It is seen in Hull town centre on 7 August 1970.

North West and Scotland

Morecambe & Heysham Corporation were in an area where almost 100 per cent AEC fleets were rare. A quick flight from nearby Blackpool to the Isle of Man where Douglas Corporation provided another similarly AEC biased fleet – with a wonderful livery too. There are more images from here than other places in this book as I stayed on the Island for several weeks during the 1970s. Lastly, there are rather pathetically few images from Scotland where I had moved house to in 1973 – but (almost) too late for Regents to be found – never a favourite type up there!

Morecambe & Heysham Corporation

The corporation maintained a small fleet of just fifty-one, 90 per cent of which were AEC. I seem to have caught them in the throes of changing their livery, with its rejection of the traditional cream. In this view of No. 55, one of the main batch of twenty-eight Regents dating from 1949 to 1954, the bus is shown in the new livery with a most peculiar advert placement. With a Park Royal body, No. 55 was from 1949 and was photographed on 25 June 1972.

No. 59 is pictured two years earlier, at Central Pier in August 1970, in its attractive old livery – with an unusual fleet number position. Another 1949 bus, this featured my favourite Park Royal body.

Also from 1949 is No. 57, which is seen in this offside view on the North Prom in August 1970.

No. 72 was a 'one-off' bus, with its RT-style side windows. From 1950, it was displayed at Earls Court when newly built. It looks smart in its newly painted livery when seen here at the station stop in August 1970.

A view from June 1972, with the rear of 1950-built No. 67 contrasting with the later style of Park Royal body fitted to 1954-built No. 79.

At least seven of the Regents from the 1949-built batch had been converted to open-top, but with garish depictions of the 'attractions' en route depicted on top-deck boards, which rather spoilt their otherwise good looks. No. 63, seen at the Park Terminus in August 1970, displays one of the least colourful!

In 1974 the corporation's fleet merged with Lancaster's, but the old liveries were retained – at least until 31 March 1975, when this view of No. 68 was obtained. The new 'City of Lancaster' name appears on the bus sides.

Douglas Corporation

Several holidays on the Isle of Man gave me the opportunity to capture more of the corporation Regents than usual, in their lovely old primrose and maroon livery. The whole fleet totalled around forty-five in the late 1960s, of which the Regents IIIs amounted to eighteen. These dated from 1947–9 and had Northern Counties bodies. Two of these are shown at the bus station on 5 August 1970, from my first (daytrip) visit. They are Nos 60 and 64 from 1948/9 and are identical – even down to the adverts.

1948-built No. 62, parked up by the bus station in August 1970, displays its distinctive Northern Counties bodywork. The shaded fleet name and numbers were a really traditional feature.

In the Regent III batch were two unusual vehicles, in that they had the London-type RT chassis, dating from 1947. The differences in appearance from the 'standard' Regent can be seen here with RT-type No. 55, which is pulling away from parked No. 60. The lower-set radiator enabled a larger windscreen to be fitted, as well as the passengers' front window. The rather archaic semaphore arm trafficator wasn't unique to the RTs, also being on the earliest 1947 'standard' Regents. It's certainly something cyclists needed to be aware of! It's a shame about the mismatched headlights – something bodybuilders often had trouble with when dealing with the RT chassis. I was lucky to see this bus as it was withdrawn later the same month, in August 1970.

A busy scene at the bus station in August 1970 with No. 59 passing No. 63 at its stop. No. 59 displays a different side window configuration, with sliding as opposed to half-drops. The sliding type were confined to a few of the earliest 1947 bodies, as was that semaphore arm trafficator, which is not very visible in this view.

1947-built No. 57 climbs a surprisingly quiet Prospect Hill, one of the shopping streets in Douglas, in August 1970.

At the bottom of the same hill, but one year later, on 30 June 1971, No. 71 – the last of the batch from 1949 –
starts its climb. This bus has more modern rounded route indicators, which were only fitted to the last two.
Note the white-coated and helmeted policeman directing traffic.

1948-built No. 61 heads along South Quay in August 1970, looking splendid in its new coat of paint. The corporation certainly kept its fleet in superb condition. The 'icing on the cake' would have been to find some triangular radiator badges, all of which are, noticeably, missing.

No. 70 (1949) leaves Ridgeway Street and turns into North Quay in June 1971.

On its way up to Douglas Head is No. 61, a 1948 bus. It is seen in June 1971.

Also seen in June 1971 at Douglas Head, No. 70 presents a different back end to the standard with flush route indicators (the built-up square boxes were usual) and rounded upper-deck back windows.

No. 70 now descends from the Head, displaying another new paint job.

Derby Castle, at one end of the proms, where 1949 No. 64 joins the Manx Electric Railway in June 1977. This is also the terminus of the horse trams.

Pictured in June 1971, 1949-built No. 64 passes the Clock Tower on Loch Prom, displaying a standard rear end. This can be compared with No. 70 on page 89.

1949-built No. 65 is seen on the proms by Villa Marina on a lovely evening in July 1971.

At Douglas railway station in June 1971 is 1949-built No. 64, fully loaded with passengers off the steam train.

No. 59, an early 1947 bus, is seen at Derby Castle terminus during June 1972. This is one of the Regents with sliding windows and that offside trafficator arm.

Four Regents (plus an Orion body) – Nos 66, 64, 63 and 60 – are lined up by the Sea Terminal to receive passengers off the Belfast ship. They were photographed in July 1976, which was to be my last image taken of the Douglas Regent IIIs.

My last trip to the island, in June 1979, found that the corporation fleet was no more – with the more modern of the corporation's buses having been incorporated into IOM National Transport. This 1968-built Regent V with a Willowbrook body, No. 37, is photographed from my hotel window on Loch Prom one early morning.

Garelochhead Coach Services, Scotland

An independent in the Helensburgh area, this company was unusual in that it purchased new double-deckers. In this view taken at Helensburgh central station in September 1975, 1966-built Regent V No. 49, with Northern Counties bodywork, is seen.

On the same day, Garellochheads No. 78 is parked at the Central station main entrance. Dating from 1968, this was the last Regent to be built.

Dundee Corporation, Scotland

Dundee was noted for its batch of thirty ex-London Craven-bodied RTs, but these had all gone by March 1969, leaving few Regents in the fleet. No. 137, with an Alexander body, and photographed at their depot in May 1973, dated from 1953 and was one of seven.

The only other Regent seen in the Dundee fleet, No. 139, from the same batch of seven, stands at the depot in May 1973.

Preserved 1930s Excellence

My very last image is a shining example of a 1934 Regent (with a Roe body); namely, Leeds No. 139, which is shown here passing through Otley on the Trans-Pennine Run in August 1985. Regent perfection!